MIXED BAG OF MAGIC TRICKS

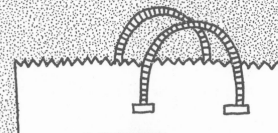

MIXED BAG OF MAGIC TRICKS

Written and Illustrated by
ROZ ABISCH and **BOCHE KAPLAN**

WALKER AND COMPANY
New York, New York

Dedication:

For Michael and Joann
at the request
of their parents
Marty and Judy Bloomberg

First published in hardcover edition in the United States of America
in 1974 by the Walker Publishing Company, Inc.

This edition published in 1984.

Trade ISBN: 0-8027-6189-5
Reinf. ISBN: 0-8027-6190-9

Library of Congress Catalog Card Number: 73-92656

Printed in the United States of America.

10 9 8 7 6 5 4 3

Table of Contents

Introduction

Magic is mysterious. Magic is amazing. Magic is fun. Magic is the art of producing wonderful results in strange and exciting ways.

You can become a magician if you learn how to use magic. With a little practice, you can be a performer who is clever enough to make the impossible seem possible.

Every magician should have a well-filled bag of tricks. Your magic bag can be an old pillowcase or a large paper sack.

Sometimes if you wear a costume it will make a trick seem more entertaining. You can make a witch's hat out of a large paper cone, or you can make a wizard's cap by pasting stars and a crescent moon on the cone. You can make an Indian turban or a gypsy headband out of a piece of colored cloth. You

7

can make a Chinese cap by pasting Oriental designs on an old beany cap. You can use almost any kind of hat: a beret, a top hat, a pirate's hat, or even a silly wig made out of yarn. Suit your costume to each trick. Place the costumes in your bag of tricks along with all the materials you plan to use during your performance.

The Performance

There are a few things to remember about giving a successful performance as a magician:
1. Practice each trick until you know it by heart if you want to impress your audience and keep their interest.
2. Prepare a "magician's patter," funny and clever things to say while you are doing your magic tricks. In addition to being entertaining, this patter will keep the audience off guard and make

your magic seem even more remarkable. Think of the patter as part of your equipment, and as you practice each trick, try to plan the words you are going to say. To start you off, most tricks in this book are introduced by a special character in a special costume with special patter.

3. Some tricks, like optical illusions (things that look different from what they really are) and static electricity tricks, are fairly easy to figure out. It would be wise to limit them to one to a performance. Don't do any trick too often, and *never* repeat any trick during the same magic show.

4. A good magician never shares his secrets. If possible, try not to tell how a trick is done.

5. Keep your act just long enough to keep the people in your audience curious and enthusiastic. When they act restless, it is time to stop.

6. Save your best trick for last so that your audience will be eager to see you perform again.

7. Magic shows are great entertainment for parties and special occasions. If your magic bag is filled and you can find a small table, you can perform anywhere and anytime. Now,

ON WITH THE SHOW.

The Snake Charmer

Tell the audience that you are an Indian snake charmer. Say, "With my magic I can make the snake come out of the basket and dance."

Reach into your bag of tricks for:

a *turban*
a *spool of thread*
a *paper cup*
a *comb*

1. Put on your turban.

2. Place the spool, with about 6″ of thread unwound, in the paper cup "basket." Allow the end of the thread to hang over the edge of the cup.

3. Go into the audience, and find someone who is wearing a sweater. Ask that person to assist you.

4. Rub the comb briskly against the sweater while your assistant counts slowly to 25.

5. Whistle your magic tune, and wave the comb over the thread in the basket.

6. The thread "snake" will rise out of the cup.

7. Move the comb slowly back and forth over the thread and the snake will dance.

8. **THE MAGIC** is in the comb and the sweater. Rubbing the comb on the sweater creates static electricity. The electricity that remains in the comb makes the thread move. This trick may take some practice because it will only work when it is done in a dry place.

The Open Door

Tell the audience that you have become known as a brilliant space engineer. Because of your very special magic power, you are the only one who can make an impossibly large object pass through an impossibly small door.

**Reach into your
bag of tricks for:**

> *a 6' tape measure*
> *a small pad of paper*
> *an index card 3" × 5"*
> *a pencil, a ruler, scissors*

1. Hold up the index card so that everyone can see it and say, "This index card represents a door."

2. Ask for a volunteer from the audience.

3. Ask the volunteer if he or she knows of any way to fit through the index card "door."

4. No matter how hard your volunteer tries, he or she will not be able to think of a way.

5. Then, with the tape measure, you compare the size of the volunteer with the size of the index card. For effect, pretend to write some complicated

figures on the pad. Hold the pad up to the audience and say, "My magic power has done it again. I will show you how to solve the problem."

6. Next, fold the index card in half so it measures 1½" × 5".

7. With the pencil and ruler, measure and mark the index card as shown, keeping each line ¼" apart.

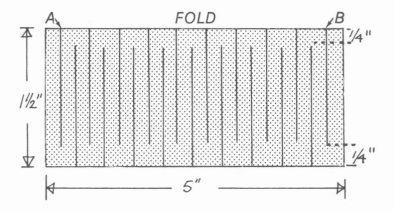

To save time, you can prepare this in advance using a second card. Show both cards to the audience so that they can see that the cards are really the same.

8. With the scissors, cut along the fold in the card from point A to point B.

9. Then, starting at point A, cut along the lines indicated from the top and the bottom of the folded card until you reach point B.

10.   Gently pull the card apart.

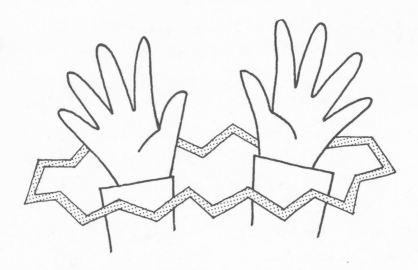

11.   The card will stretch into a door large enough for your volunteer to fit through.

12.   **THE MAGIC** is in the way you measure and cut the card. If you follow instructions, the card will open up to form a large, continuous zigzag band.

Toothpick Teasers

Now say, "In my magic experiments as an engineer, I have discovered several remarkable ways to re-arrange space."

**Reach into your
bag of tricks for:**

a box of wooden toothpicks

TEASER NUMBER ONE

1. Take 16 toothpicks out of the box.

2. Use the 16 toothpicks to make 5 squares as shown.

3. Ask for a volunteer from the audience.

4. Say to your volunteer, "I want you to make 4 squares out of the 5 by rearranging only 3 toothpicks."

5. **THE MAGIC** is in the 3 toothpicks. Remove toothpicks A, B, and C.

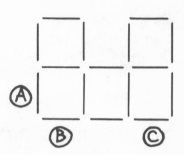

6. Set them in place as shown below.

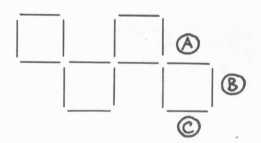

TEASER NUMBER TWO

1. Arrange 16 toothpicks to form 2 squares.

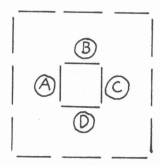

2. Ask for a volunteer from the audience.
    Give him or her 2 more toothpicks.

3. Say, "I want you to make 3 squares out of the 2 you have made by using only 2 more toothpicks."

4. **THE MAGIC** is in re-arranging the tooth-picks in the center square. See the illus-tration.

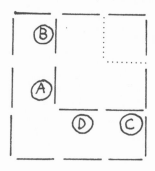

TEASER NUMBER THREE

1. Set out 15 toothpicks as shown.

2. Say, "Is there anyone in the audience who is good at arithmetic?"

3. Choose a volunteer, and then ask, "Can you remove 6 toothpicks and still leave 10?"

4. **THE MAGIC** is in removing only the toothpicks shown in dashes. See the illustration.

Instant Surgery

You are a skilled surgeon. You have just perfected the first do-it-yourself operation.

**Reach into your
bag of tricks for:**

> *a surgical mask*
> *a toy stethoscope*
> *a pad of paper 8½" × 11"*

1. Put on the surgical mask, and hang the stethoscope around your neck.

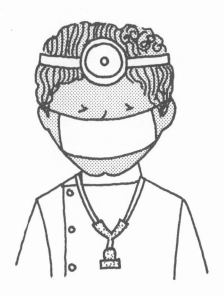

2. Hand a piece of paper to each person in the audience.

3. Ask everyone to roll the paper into a 1″ tube.

4. Tell everyone to keep both eyes wide open. Then ask each one to hold the tube up to his or her right eye.

5. At the same time, each one is to hold his or her left hand up vertically alongside the end of the tube.

6. Almost immediately, each one in the audience will see a hole in his or her left hand.

7. *THE MAGIC* is in the eyes and the mind. Each eye sees a separate image. Because the hole in the tube and the left hand are so close to the eyes, the mind cannot combine them into a single picture. The hole that appears in the hand is called an *optical illusion*.

Optical Illusions

Optical illusions are a lot of fun. But some people can figure them out quite easily, so try to use only one during a performance. Here are several optical illusions to try on your audience. You can prepare them ahead of time by drawing them on a large piece of paper or cardboard.

To introduce an optical illusion you can hold up your hand and ask, "How many fingers do you see?" When someone in the audience calls out, "Five," say, "Are you sure? Do you really think you can believe your eyes?" Then show one of the following optical illusions and see what happens.

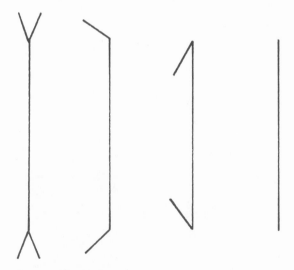

1. Is any one of these vertical lines longer than the others?

   They are all the same length.

2. Is either of these circles larger than the other?

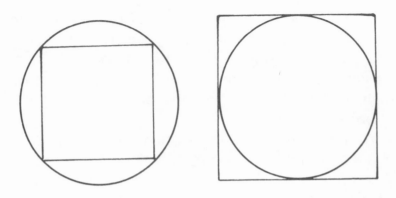

They are both the same size.

3. Which circle looks smaller?

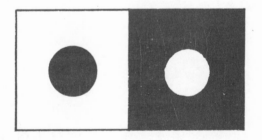

They are both the same size.

22

4. Is this magician's hat higher than it is wide?

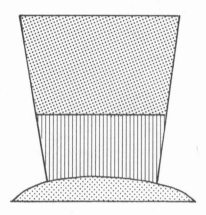

The height is the same as the width.

5. Do you think this fan forms a perfect circle?

It does.

The Forgetful Chef

Introduce yourself to the audience. Say, "I am Fran the Fantastic, the famous French chef." Tell the audience that in addition to being fancy and fabulous, you are also so forgetful that you keep getting your hard-boiled eggs mixed in with your raw eggs.

Reach into your bag of tricks for:

*an apron
a chef's hat
a small bowl
3 raw eggs
1 hard-boiled egg
1 flat tray*

1. Place the chef's hat on your head, and put on the apron.

2. Place all the eggs in the bowl.

3. Tell the audience that you've gotten one hard-boiled egg mixed in with the raw eggs.

4. Ask for 4 volunteers from the audience to help you find the hard-boiled egg.

5. Tell one volunteer to hold the tray level and steady.

6. Hand one egg to each of the other volunteers, and keep the last egg for yourself.

7. Say, "Let's start all four eggs spinning on the tray at the same time." Watch the eggs very closely.

8. Then pick up one egg and crack it to show everyone that it is hard boiled.

9. **THE MAGIC** is in the eggs. The raw eggs will stop spinning because of the friction created by the liquid inside the shells. The hard-boiled eggs will continue to spin much faster and much longer.

The Flying Egg

For this trick you can still wear your chef's cap and apron.

Reach into your bag of tricks for:

an egg cup
a hard-boiled egg

1. Place the hard-boiled egg, narrow end down, in the egg cup.

2. Show the egg and the egg cup to the audience and say, "Here I have one hard-boiled egg and one egg cup."

3. Tell the audience you are going to *fly* an egg.

4. Bring the egg cup close to your mouth.

5. Blow air into the egg cup between the egg and the top of the cup.

6. Blow very, very hard, and the egg will fly out of the cup.

7. **THE MAGIC** is in the air you blow into the egg cup. As air pressure is increased under the egg, the egg will be lifted out of the cup.

A Hair Raiser

You are a scary witch. By your own special magic you can make hair stand on end.

**Reach into your
bag of tricks for:**

> *a witch's hat*
> *a pencil*
> *a piece of paper 4½" × 12"*
> *a watch*

1. Put on your witch's hat.

2. Tell the audience that you have the power to make hair stand on end.

3. Ask for two volunteers.

4. Place the paper on a table, and rub the pencil over it briskly for 30 seconds. Ask one of the volunteers to time you with the watch.

5. After the 30 seconds are up, hold the paper over the head of the second volunteer. His hair will stand on end.

6. ***THE MAGIC*** is in the rubbing. When the pencil is rubbed against the paper it creates static electricity. The electricity that remains in the paper makes the hair stand up. Be sure not to do more than one static electricity trick during any performance, because they are easy to figure out.

The Right Date

You are a very efficient executive. You have devised a formula that always gives you the right date.

**Reach into your
bag of tricks for:**

> *a pair of eyeglasses*
> *a pad*
> *2 pencils*
> *a calendar*

1. Ask for a volunteer from the audience.

2. Give that person the calendar and the pencil.

```
        JANUARY
 S  M  T  W  T  F  S
          1  2  3  4  5  6
 7  8  9 10 11 12 13
14 (15)(16)(17) 18 19 20
21 22 23 24 25 26 27
28 29 30 31
```

3. Tell the volunteer to circle 3 consecutive numbers on the calendar and then give you the sum of those numbers.

4. Put on the eyeglasses. Write the total sum on your pad. Then tell your audience exactly which dates were circled.

5. **THE MAGIC** is in the numbers. To get the answer, divide the total by 3 to find the center date. Subtract 1 from the center date to find the first date, and add 1 to the center date to find the last date.

The Name Dropper

You are gifted with great powers of concentration. Tell the audience that your keen mind can guide you even when you are not able to see.

**Reach into your
bag of tricks for:**

> *a piece of paper 8½" × 11"*
> *9 pencils*
> *a hat*
> *a blindfold*

1. Hold up the piece of paper so that it can be seen by everyone in the audience. Show the audience that both sides of the paper are blank.

2. Fold the paper into thirds and then into thirds again. Now it is divided into 9 equal sections.

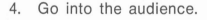

3. Tear the 9 sections apart.

4. Go into the audience.

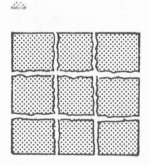

5. Hand a pencil and a section of the paper to 9 people. As you do so, ask each person her or his name.

6. Tell each one to write her or his name on the paper and fold it in half.

7. Choose an assistant from the audience. Tell your assistant to tie the blindfold on you. Ask her or him to collect all the folded pieces of paper, place them in the hat, and mix them up thoroughly.

8. With the blindfold on, pull one piece of paper out of the hat. Hold the paper up to show everyone that it is still folded in half. Announce the name that is written on the paper.

9. Hand the paper to your assistant. Ask him to tell the audience the name that is written on it. It is sure to be the name you mentioned.

10. *THE MAGIC* is in the piece of paper, your memory, and your fingertips. The way the paper is folded and torn, only the center section will have four rough edges. Remember the name of the person to whom you give that one piece of paper. When you reach into the hat, feel for the rough edges, and you will always amaze your audience. Because this trick will only work with certain types of paper, you may have to experiment until you find the right kind.

The Undecided Tourist

You are a worldly traveler. You have visited so many different exciting places that you cannot decide where to go next.

**Reach into your
bag of tricks for:**

> *a map of the world*
> *a small pad of paper*
> *a pencil*
> *a hat*

1. Hold up the map of the world.

2. Ask the audience to help you decide upon which place to see.

3. Pretend to write each suggestion down on a separate piece of paper, but really write the name of the first place that is suggested on each piece.

4. Fold each piece of paper, and place it in the hat.

5. Select a volunteer from the audience. Ask that person, as your assistant, to mix up the pieces of paper in the hat.

6. Draw one piece of paper out of the hat, and hand it to your assistant.

7. Tear the rest of the papers into little pieces, and discard them.

8. Think for a moment, then tell the audience the name of the place that is written on the piece of paper being held by your assistant.

9. **THE MAGIC** is in the name of the first place mentioned. You have written that place down on each slip of paper, and your answer has to be right.

Concentration

Tell the audience that you can project very powerful thought waves. By concentrating very hard, you can make people do exactly what you wish.

**Reach into your
bag of tricks for:**

> a *deck of cards*
> a *small piece of paper*
> a *pencil*

1. Ask for a volunteer from the audience.

2. Set two small piles of cards on the table.

3. Tell the audience that you will use thought waves to make your assistant choose between the two piles.

4. Make a note of the pile to be chosen on the piece of paper. Fold the paper, and hand it to your assistant.

5. Ask your assistant to pick up one of the piles and compare the cards to the number you have written on the paper.

6. The numbers will be the same.

7. **THE MAGIC** is in the note and the cards. You have written the number 5 on the paper. One pile of cards is made up of four 5's, and the other pile is made of 5 cards. In advance, prepare two piles of cards. One pile should contain 4 cards, all 5's. The other pile should contain 5 cards. Therefore, if you write the number 5 on the paper, your answer will be right no matter which pile is chosen.

The Diamond Discovery

Tell the audience that your power of concentration is becoming stronger and stronger. It is so powerful that you are able to identify a card that has been picked while you were out of the room.

**Reach into your
bag of tricks for:**

a deck of cards

1. Pick an assistant from the audience.

2. Give your assistant the deck of cards. Tell him or her to deal 10 cards onto the table after you leave the room. The cards are to be placed on the table face up.

3. While you are out of the room, your assistant asks someone to come out of the audience and point to 1 of the 10 cards. The audience is told which card has been chosen.

4. When you return, tell everyone that your remarkable power of concentration is directing you to a specific card. Then name the card.

5. ***THE MAGIC*** is in the cards and your assistant. The assistant you choose will really be a friend with whom you've practiced the trick in advance.

Here's how the trick works: your assistant lays out the cards in the pattern shown below. This pattern is the same as the markings on the 10 of diamonds. Be sure to include a 10 of diamonds in the cards that are used.

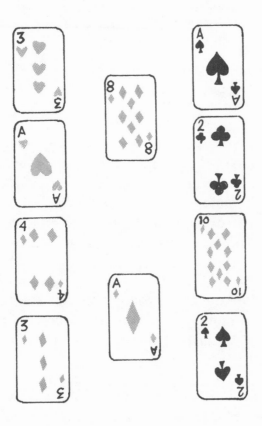

When you return, your assistant will secretly point to the diamond on the 10 of diamonds which will indicate the position of the card selected while you were out of the room.

Correct Spelling

You are a wizard at spelling. For some mysterious reason it is impossible for you to make any mistakes. Say to the audience, "I have a feeling that some of you don't believe me. Well, if you wait a moment, I'll prove it to you."

**Reach into your
bag of tricks for:**

> a *wizard's cap*
> a *small pack of 13 cards*
> *all in the same suit: ACE,
> TWO, THREE, FOUR, FIVE, SIX, SEVEN,
> EIGHT, NINE, TEN, JACK, QUEEN, KING.*

1. Put on the wizard's cap.

2. Show the pack of cards to the audience.

3. Tell the audience you are going to find and name every card in the pack without looking at any of the cards.

4. Hold the cards face down. Say, "A," and slip the top card to the bottom of the pack.

5. Say "C," and place the next card under the pack.

6. Say, "E," and place the third card under the pack.

7. Hold up the next card. It will be the ACE.

8. In the same manner, continue to spell out the rest of the cards in order: TWO, THREE, FOUR, FIVE, SIX, SEVEN, EIGHT, NINE, TEN, JACK, QUEEN, KING. You will always come up with the card you spelled out.

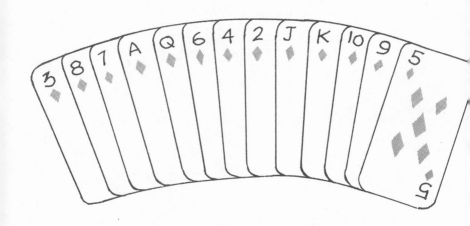

9. **THE MAGIC** is in the cards. They must be arranged in this special way for the trick to work, so be very careful when you set up the cards.

The Age Detector

Tell the audience that you are a very clever detective. Say, "It is not always easy to tell a person's age by how he or she looks. It has taken many years and a lot of research, but I have finally succeeded in developing a foolproof method which can determine anyone's age."

**Reach into your
bag of tricks for:**

a *detective's cap*
a *magnifying glass*
a *piece of paper*
a *pencil*

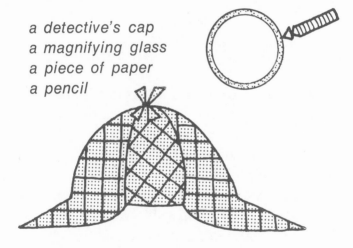

1.   Put on the detective's cap.

2.   Use your magnifying glass to inspect the audience.

3.   Stop in front of someone you do not know and hand that person the paper and pencil.

4. Ask the person to think of the months in terms of numbers. For example:

JANUARY 1
FEBRUARY 2
MARCH 3
APRIL 4
MAY 5
JUNE 6
JULY 7
AUGUST 8
SEPTEMBER 9
OCTOBER 10
NOVEMBER . . . 11
DECEMBER . . . 12

5. Then tell the person to do the following:
   A. Multiply the number of his or her birth month by 2.
   B. To that number, add 5.
   C. Multiply the total by 50.
   D. To that total, add his or her age.
   E. From that total, subtract 365.
   F. To that sum, add 115.

6. Ask for the final total. From the first number, or the first two numbers, you will be able to tell in what month the person was born. The last two numbers will tell you how old he or she is.

7. **THE MAGIC** is in the numbers. For example if a
    10-year-old was born in March, the formula would
    work as follows:

$$MARCH = 3$$

$$
\begin{array}{r}
3 \times 2 = 6 \\
+\,5 \\
\hline
11 \\
\times 50 \\
\hline
550 \\
+\,10 \\
\hline
560 \\
-365 \\
\hline
195 \\
+115 \\
\hline
310
\end{array}
$$

The 3 refers to March.
The 10 states his or
her age.

It would be a good idea to practice this trick many
times so that you can do it correctly and very quickly
during a performance.

The Lucky Number

Keep on your detective's cap. Tell the audience, "I have another magic formula that will reveal the age of a person I don't know."

Reach into your
bag of tricks for:

> *a pencil*
> *a piece of paper*

1. Find someone in the audience that you do not know. If you know everyone, it might be best to go on to another trick. Just say, "I think I'll go on to another trick, because there is no one here that I do not know."

2. Give the person you do not know the pencil and paper. Then say:
   A. "Please write your age on the paper."
   B. "My lucky number is 90. Add my lucky number to your age."
   C. "Cross out the first number on the left side of the total."
   D. "Add that number to the remaining sum."
   E. "Now, tell the audience the final sum."

3. In your head, quickly add 9 to the final total. Then tell the audience how old the person is.

4. **THE MAGIC** is in the numbers.
   For example:

A. If the person in the audience is _____ 13

B. Add the lucky number _____ 90

$$\overline{103}$$

C. Cross out the first number on the left
   and add it to the total _____
$$\require{cancel}\cancel{1}03$$
$$+1$$
$$\overline{4}$$

D. You add 9 to the total _____
$$+9$$
$$\overline{13}$$

E. To get the person's age _____ 13

The Color Clue

You are a famous creative artist. You are so sensitive to colors that you can identify them even when you are blindfolded.

**Reach into your
bag of tricks for:**

> *a beret*
> *an artist's smock*
> *a box of assorted crayons (very waxy)*
> *a blindfold*

1. Put on your beret and artist's smock.

2. Ask for a volunteer from the audience to act as your assistant.

3. Tell your assistant to tie the blindfold on you.

4. Direct your assistant to go into the audience and have someone take one crayon out of the box.

5. Ask your assistant to bring that crayon to you.

6. Pass the crayon through your hands. Then have your assistant return the crayon to the box.

7. Remove the blindfold, and pretend to concentrate for a minute. Then name the color of the crayon.

8. *THE MAGIC* is in the crayon and your thumbnail. When you pass the crayon through your hands, scrape the crayon with your thumbnail. When you pretend to concentrate, raise your hand slowly and rub it across your forehead. As you raise your hand, peek at the color under your nail. Not all crayons will work for this trick. Try several kinds in order to find those that work best. This trick also requires quite a bit of practice before you can perform it with ease.

The Dollar Robbery

You are a clever thief. You are so light-fingered that you never drop anything or leave fingerprints behind.

**Reach into your
bag of tricks for:**

> a *thief's mask with
> openings to see through*
> a *dollar bill*
> a *drinking glass*

1. Put on the mask.

2. Ask for two volunteers from the audience.

3. Give the dollar bill to one of them, and say, "Please place the dollar bill on the table."

4. Give the glass to the other volunteer, and say, "Please place the glass on top of the dollar bill."

5. Tell the audience that you will steal the money without lifting or touching the glass with your hands.

6. **THE MAGIC** is in the dollar bill and your fingers. Hold the bill at one of the narrow ends. Using both hands, slowly begin to roll it up. Be sure to keep your fingers away from the glass. As the bill is rolled up it will push the glass off. Then you will be able to remove it without touching anything else.

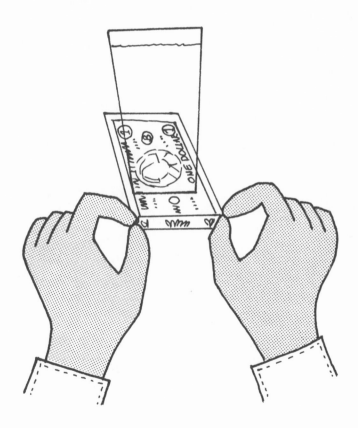

The Penny Mystery

Tell the audience that you are a great mind reader. Then say, "I can pick the mystery penny out of the hat even when I am blindfolded."

**Reach into your
bag of tricks for:**

> *a hat*
> *6 copper pennies with different dates*
> *a blindfold*

1. Put the pennies in the hat.

2. Choose an assistant from the audience.

3. Ask your assistant to tie the blindfold over your eyes.

4. Say, "Will someone else in the audience please take one penny out of the hat and memorize the date on the coin?"

5. Have the penny passed around the room, and ask each person to remember the date, too.

6. Have the last person place the penny back in the hat. Ask your assistant to place the hat in your hand.

7. Even though you are blindfolded you will pick the right penny.

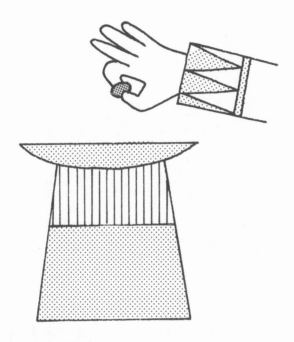

8. *THE MAGIC* is in the penny. Copper is a good conductor of heat. The mystery penny will become warm from handling and will be easy to find among the rest. Because copper is a good conductor of heat, it is best to do this trick in a cool place so that only the penny that is passed around from hand to hand will get warm.

The Magic Marbles

Tell the audience that you have found a bag of magic marbles. Say, "I am going to show you how my magic marbles multiply."

**Reach into your
bag of tricks for:**

a bag of marbles

1. Take out one marble. Hold it up and ask, "How many marbles do you see?"

2. Someone will say, "One marble." Ask that person to be your assistant.

3. Place the marble on a table.

4. Tell your assistant to cross the middle finger of his or her right hand over the index finger.

5. Say to your assistant, "Close your eyes and gently rub the marble under your crossed fingertips."

6. Then ask, "How many marbles do you feel?"

7. Your assistant will feel 2 marbles under his or her fingertips.

8. ***THE MAGIC*** is in the fingertips and the mind. When the fingers are crossed, the nerve passages to the brain are crossed. Each finger feels the marble separately, so it feels like 2 marbles.

Button, Button Number 1

You are a button collector. Say to the audience, "When I was little, I always lost my buttons, so I decided to collect them. Now I am the World Champion Button Collector, and I know of different ways to use them."

**Reach into your
bag of tricks for:**

> *a few boxes of mixed buttons
> an index card 3″ × 5″
> 4 drinking straws about 8¼″ long*

1. Ask for a volunteer from the audience to be your assistant.

2. Tell your assistant to hunt through the button boxes for 9 identical flat buttons.

3. Tell him or her to set the buttons out on the index card in 3 equally spaced rows as shown.

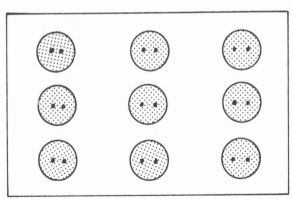

4. Then say, "Please place the drinking straws on the 9 buttons in such a way that all of the buttons will be covered and each straw is touching the other 3 straws."

5. **THE MAGIC** is in the buttons and the straws. The straws must be placed on the buttons as shown in the illustration.

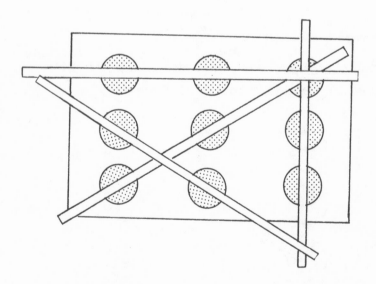

Button, Button Number 2

1. Ask for a volunteer from the audience.

2. Ask the volunteer to look through the button boxes to find 10 flat buttons all the same size. These are to be placed on a table.

3. After the buttons are on the table, say to the volunteer, "Please try to place the 10 buttons in 5 rows of 4 buttons each."

4. Then say to the audience, "Let us count to 20 very quietly to see how quickly the trick can be done."

5. Your volunteer will not be able to work out the trick in so short a time. This trick can keep you busy for a long time if you do not know the magic.

6. **THE MAGIC** is in the arrangement of the buttons. For the trick to work, the 10 buttons have to be arranged in the star pattern shown in the illustration.

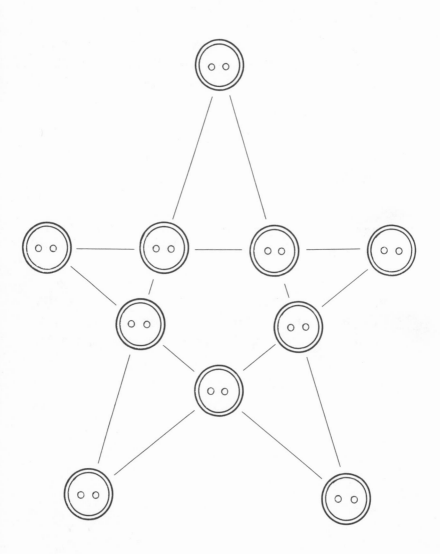

The Magic Knot

You are a salty old sailor. Because you are too old to climb the rigging and too weak to raise the sails, the captain has appointed you to be in charge of ropes and knot-tying. Say to the audience, "I have spent so much time tying knots that I have found one that works like magic."

Reach into your bag of tricks for:

> *a sailor's cap*
> *4 pieces of string about 2' long*

1. Put on the sailor's cap.

2. Ask for 3 volunteers from the audience.

3. Give each volunteer a piece of string.

4. Ask each of them to try to tie a knot in the string without letting go of the ends.

5. No one will be able to do it.

6. Next, show the audience how to tie the knot.

7. **THE MAGIC** is in your arms. A knot will be tied as if by magic if you do the following:

    A.   Lay the string out on a table.
    B.   Cross your arms.
    C.   Bend over the string.
    D.   Grab one end of the string with each hand.
    E.   Straighten up and uncross your arms. The knot will be tied.

THIS HAND PICKS UP THIS END OF THE STRING

THIS HAND PICKS UP THIS END OF THE STRING

The Mystic Charm

You have been given a rare Egyptian charm. It is so old that it has fallen apart. The only way you can use its magic is if you put it back together again.

**Reach into your
bag of tricks for:**

an envelope marked MYSTIC CHARM

1. Ask for a volunteer from the audience.

2. Give the volunteer the envelope marked MYSTIC CHARM. The envelope will contain these 4 pieces of cardboard.

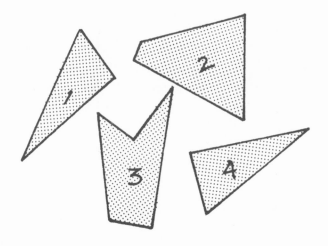

3. Ask your volunteer to try to arrange the pieces into the shape of a diamond.

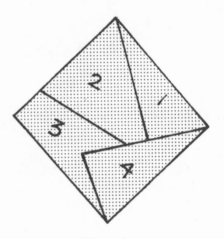

4. **THE MAGIC** is in the numbered pieces of cardboard. The illustration shows the way the shapes will look when the cardboard pieces are put together properly.